Reading for Meaning
Grade 1
Table of Contents

FS-11045 Homework Helpers—Reading for Meaning 1
All rights reserved—Printed in the U.S.A.
Copyright © 1995 Frank Schaffer Publications, Inc.
23740 Hawthorne Blvd., Torrance, CA 90505

ISBN #0-86734-814-3

This book is a compilation of Frank Schaffer's
Boxed Activity Cards FS-3138.

My Dog

Read the story.
Answer each question.
Write a complete sentence.

My dog, Wags, ran fast.
He ran after the cat.

1. What is the dog's name?

2. Did the dog run?

3. Did the dog run after a boy?

4. What did the dog run after?

5. Is the dog a boy dog or a girl dog?

Write your answers below.

FS-11045 Homework Helpers—Reading for Meaning 1

My Monster

Read the story.
Answer each question.
Write a complete sentence.

My monster has a big red hat.
A flower is on the hat.

1. What does my monster have?

2. Is the hat big or little?

3. What color is the hat?

4. Is a cat on the hat?

5. What is on the hat?

Write your answers below.

FS-11045 Homework Helpers—Reading for Meaning 1

Jim's Blocks

Read the story. Answer each question.
Write a complete sentence.

Jim plays with big blocks.
The blocks are made of wood.
Jim makes trains and trucks.

1. Who plays with blocks?

2. Are the blocks big or little?

3. What are the blocks made of?

4. Did Jim make a house?

5. What did Jim make?

Write your answers below.

Two Mice

Read the story. Answer each question.
Write a complete sentence.

Jane saw two mice.
The mice were gray.
They ate cheese and nuts.

1. What did Jane see?

2. How many mice did Jane see?

3. Were the mice white?

4. Did the mice eat cheese?

5. What else did the mice eat?

Write your answers below.

The Little Monkey

Read the story. Answer each question.
Write a complete sentence.

The little monkey has fun.
She plays all day.
She lives in the zoo.

1. Who is this story about?

2. Is the monkey big?

3. When does the monkey play?

4. Where does the monkey live?

5. Does the monkey have fun?

Write your answers below.

FS-11045 Homework Helpers—Reading for Meaning 1

The Elephant

Read the story. Answer each question.
Write a complete sentence.

The elephant is big and gray.
His trunk is long.
His ears are wide.

1. Who is this story about?

2. Is the elephant big or little?

3. What color is the elephant?

4. What is long?

5. What are wide?

Write your answers below.

Maria's Bike

Read the story. Answer each question.
Write a complete sentence.

Maria has a new bike.
It has two wheels.
It is blue.

1. Who has a bike?

2. Is the bike old or new?

3. Does the bike have three wheels?

4. How many wheels does the bike have?

5. What color is the bike?

Write your answers below.

FS-11045 Homework Helpers—Reading for Meaning 1

The Funny Clown

Read the story. Answer each question.
Write a complete sentence.

A funny clown came to school.
She came on Monday.
She had six balloons.

1. Who came to school?

2. Was she sad or funny?

3. What day did she come?

4. Was the clown a boy?

5. What did the clown have?

Write your answers below.

FS-11045 Homework Helpers—Reading for Meaning 1

Nancy's Hamster

Read the story. Answer each question.
Write a complete sentence.

Nancy has a brown hamster.
The hamster has a little wheel.
Nancy loves the hamster.

1. Who has a hamster?

2. What color is the hamster?

3. Who has a wheel?

4. Is the wheel big or little?

5. Who loves the hamster?

Write your answers below.

Tom's Cat

Read the story. Answer each question.
Write a complete sentence.

Tom's brown cat ran away.
It came back after five days.
Tom was so glad!

1. What color is Tom's cat?

2. What did the cat do?

3. Did it come back after one day?

4. When did it come back?

5. Was Tom glad to see the cat?

Write your answers below.

Sue's Snake

Read the story. Answer each question.
Write a complete sentence.

Sue has a pet snake.
It is in a green box.
The box has a top.

1. Who has a pet?

2. What is the pet?

3. Is the pet in a tree?

4. What color is the box?

5. Does the box have a top?

Write your answers below.

_____

_____

_____

_____

_____

_____

_____

_____

The Ball Game

Read the story. Answer each question.
Write a complete sentence.

Joan and Frank played a ball game.
They played at the park.
They played on Saturday.

1. Who played with Joan?

2. What did they play?

3. Where did they play?

4. Did they play on Monday?

5. When did they play?

Write your answers below.

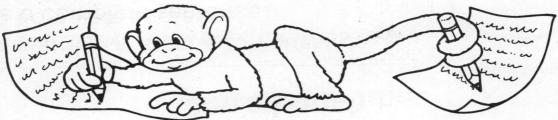

Jim's Lunch

Read the story. Answer each question.
Write a complete sentence.

Jim ate an apple.
It was big and red.
It was in his lunchbox.

1. Who ate something?

2. What color was it?

3. Was it big or little?

4. What did Jim eat?

5. Where was the apple?

Write your answers below.

Pull-Out Answers

Page 1
1. The dog's name is Wags.
2. Yes, the dog ran.
3. No, the dog did not run after a boy.
4. The dog ran after a cat.
5. The dog is a boy dog.

Page 2
1. The monster has a big red hat.
2. The hat is big.
3. The hat is red.
4. No, a cat is not on the hat.
5. A flower is on the hat.

Page 3
1. Jim plays with blocks.
2. The blocks are big.
3. The blocks are made of wood.
4. No, Jim did not make a house.
5. Jim made trains and trucks.

Page 4
1. Jane saw mice.
2. Jane saw two mice.
3. No, the mice were not white.
4. Yes, the mice ate cheese.
5. The mice ate nuts.

Page 5
1. This story is about a monkey.
2. No, the monkey is not big.
3. The monkey plays all day.
4. The monkey lives in the zoo.
5. Yes, the monkey has fun.

Page 6
1. The story is about an elephant.
2. The elephant is big.
3. The elephant is gray.
4. The elephant's trunk is long.
5. The elephant's ears are wide.

Page 7
1. Maria has a bike.
2. The bike is new.
3. No, the bike does not have three wheels.
4. The bike has two wheels.
5. The bike is blue.

Page 8
1. A funny clown came to school.
2. She was funny.
3. She came on Monday.
4. No, the clown was not a boy.
5. The clown had six balloons.

Page 9
1. Nancy has a hamster.
2. The hamster is brown.
3. The hamster has a wheel.
4. The wheel is little.
5. Nancy loves the hamster.

Pull-Out Answers

Page 10
1. Tom's cat is brown.
2. The cat ran away.
3. No, it did not come back after one day.
4. It came back after five days.
5. Yes, Tom was glad to see the cat.

Page 11
1. Sue has a pet.
2. The pet is a snake.
3. No, the pet is not in a tree.
4. The box is green.
5. Yes, the box has a top.

Page 12
1. Frank played with Joan.
2. They played a ball game.
3. They played at the park.
4. No, they did not play on Monday.
5. They played on Saturday.

Page 13
1. Jim ate something.
2. It was red.
3. It was big.
4. Jim ate an apple.
5. The apple was in his lunchbox.

Page 14
1. Carlo is a boy.
2. Carlo went to a park.
3. No, he did not play on the slide.
4. He played on the swings.
5. Carlo jumped into the pool.

Page 15
1. Dana has skates.
2. She skates every day.
3. Dana is a girl.
4. Her dog runs after her.
5. The dog does not skate.

Page 16
1. The pig's name is Pinky Pig.
2. He lives on a farm.
3. He is pink.
4. His is fat.
5. He eats apples.

Page 17
1. It rained.
2. A rainbow is in the sky.
3. Yes, the rainbow has an end.
4. The rainbow ends in the lake.
5. This will be a lucky day.

Page 18
1. It is sunny.
2. Yes, we will take a walk.
3. We will go to the library.
4. We will read books at the library.
5. We will bring home a storybook.

Pull-Out Answers

Page 19
1. Ivan can write the alphabet.
2. Ivan can tie his shoes.
3. Five and five are ten.
4. Ivan is learning to ride a two-wheel bike.
5. No, his bike does not have three wheels.

Page 20
1. Mia's birthday is today.
2. Mia will have a party at her house.
3. The balloons are red and green.
4. Yes, she will have a birthday cake.
5. There will be seven candles on the cake.

Page 21
1. I see color everywhere.
2. The grass is green.
3. The sky is blue.
4. The car is red.
5. The red car is going fast.

Page 22
1. Yes, it snowed last night.
2. Snow covers the house.
3. Yes, there are trees outside.
4. The trees are white.
5. It is cold outside.

Page 23
1. Ned sees many things in the sky.
2. Ned sees a moon and stars at bedtime.
3. He sees the sun and clouds at noon.
4. He sees birds at dinnertime.
5. The birds are red and blue.

Page 24
1. Your plants grow in your garden.
2. Tomatoes are red.
3. Yes, you grow carrots.
4. Yes, you grow something in the spring.
5. You grow strawberries in the spring.

Page 25
1. Wiggle is a worm.
2. He is hard to hold because he wiggles.
3. He lives in a little box.
4. The box is yellow.
5. No, Wiggle does not make a sound.

HOMEWORK AWARD
presented to

_____

for successfully completing
this Homework Helper Book

_____
signed

_____
date

D

FS-11045 Homework Helpers—Reading for Meaning 1

The Park

Read the story. Answer each question.
Write a complete sentence.

Carlo went to a park.
He played on the swings.
He jumped into the pool.
He did not go on the slide.

1. Is Carlo a boy or a girl?

2. Where did Carlo go?

3. Did he play on the slide?

4. What did he play on?

5. Where did Carlo jump?

Write your answers below.

boilerplate
© Frank Schaffer Publications, Inc.

FS-11045 Homework Helpers—Reading for Meaning 1

Skates

Read the story. Answer each question.
Write a complete sentence.

Dana has skates.
She skates every day.
Her dog runs after her.
It does not skate.

1. What does Dana have?

2. When does she skate?

3. Is Dana a girl or a boy?

4. Who runs after her?

5. Who does not skate?

Write your answers below.

FS-11045 Homework Helpers—Reading for Meaning 1

Pinky Pig

Read the story. Answer each question.
Write a complete sentence.

Pinky Pig lives on a farm.
He is pink.
He is fat.
He eats apples.

1. What is the pig's name?

2. Where does he live?

3. What color is he?

4. Is he fat or thin?

5. What does he eat?

Write your answers below.

_____

_____

_____

_____

_____

_____

_____

_____

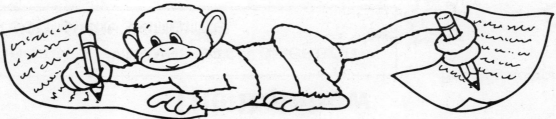

The Rainbow

Read the story. Answer each question.
Write a complete sentence.

It just rained.
A rainbow is in the sky.
The end of the rainbow is in the lake.
This will be a lucky day.

1. Did it rain or snow?

2. What is in the sky?

3. Does the rainbow have an end?

4. Where does the rainbow end?

5. What kind of day will this be?

Write your answers below.

FS-11045 Homework Helpers—Reading for Meaning 1

A Walk

Read the story. Answer each question.
Write a complete sentence.

The sun is out.
Let's take a walk to the library.
We will read books there.
We will bring a storybook home.

1. Is it sunny or rainy?

2. Will we take a walk?

3. Where will we go?

4. What will we do at the library?

5. What will we bring home?

Check Out Books
Here

Write your answers below.

Look at Ivan

Read the story. Answer each question.
Write a complete sentence.

Ivan can write the alphabet.
He can tie his shoes.
He knows that five and five make ten.
He is learning to ride a two-wheel bike.

1. What can Ivan write?

2. What can Ivan tie?

3. How much are five and five?

4. What is Ivan learning?

5. Does Ivan's bike have three wheels?

Write your answers below.

Happy Birthday

> Read the story. Answer each question.
> Write a complete sentence.

Today is Mia's birthday.
She will have a party at her house.
There will be red and green balloons.
The cake will have seven candles.

1. When is Mia's birthday?

2. What will Mia have at her house?

3. What colors are the balloons?

4. Will she have a birthday cake?

5. How many candles will be on the cake?

Write your answers below.

Color Is Everywhere

Read the story. Answer each question.
Write a complete sentence.

Everywhere you look you see color.
The grass is green.
The sky is blue.
A red car is going fast.

1. What do you see everywhere?

2. What is green?

3. What color is the sky?

4. What is red?

5. What is going fast?

Write your answers below.

FS-11045 Homework Helpers—Reading for Meaning 1

Snow

Read the story. Answer each question.
Write a complete sentence.

Snow fell last night.
The house is covered with snow.
The trees are white.
It is cold outside.

1. Did it snow last night?

2. What covers the house?

3. Are there trees outside?

4. What color are the trees?

5. Is it hot or cold outside?

Write your answers below.

_____

_____

_____

_____

_____

_____

_____

_____

22

The Sky

Read the story. Answer each question.
Write a complete sentence.

Ned sees many things in the sky.
At bedtime he sees a moon and stars.
At noon he sees the sun and clouds.
At dinnertime he sees red and blue birds.

1. Where does Ned see many things?

2. What does Ned see at bedtime?

3. When does he see the sun and clouds?

4. When does he see birds?

5. What colors are the birds?

Write your answers below.

FS-11045 Homework Helpers—Reading for Meaning 1

Our Garden

Read the story. Answer each question.
Write a complete sentence.

We grow many plants in our garden.
We grow red tomatoes.
We grow lots of carrots.
In the spring we pick strawberries.

1. Where do our plants grow?

2. What is red?

3. Do we grow carrots?

4. Do we grow something in the spring?

5. What do we grow in the spring?

Write your answers below.

FS-11045 Homework Helpers—Reading for Meaning 1

Wiggle Worm

Read the story. Answer each question.
Write a complete sentence.

Wiggle is a pet worm.
He is hard to hold because he wiggles.
He lives in a little yellow box.
He never makes a sound.

1. Who is Wiggle?

2. Why is he hard to hold?

3. Where does he live?

4. What color is the box?

5. Does Wiggle make a sound?

Write your answers below.

FS-11045 Homework Helpers—Reading for Meaning 1

Homework Helper Record

Color the star for each page you complete.